THE
TABLA
Book of New Verse

THE
TABLA
Book of New Verse

EDITOR
Stephen James

EDITORIAL ADDRESS
The Tabla Book of New Verse
The Department of English
The University of Bristol
3-5 Woodland Road
Bristol BS8 1TB

E-MAIL
stephen.james@bristol.ac.uk

WEBSITE
www.bristol.ac.uk/tabla

FAX
0117 928 8860

PUBLISHING ASSISTANTS
Jess Dunton
Philippa Nokes

DESIGNED BY
Gideon Tearle

PRINTED AND BOUND BY
ColourBooks Ltd

Copies of this book may be purchased direct from the editorial address. The cost per book is £6.00 (post free) or £8.00 to libraries and institutions. For overseas orders, please add £1.00 (Europe) or £2.00 (rest of world). Cheques and postal orders should be made payable to *Tabla*. Only UK sterling payments can be accepted.

Poets seeking publication are requested to approach *The Tabla Book of New Verse* through the tie-in competition in the first instance. Details of this are provided towards the back of the book. Those whose work is accepted for next year's anthology will also be invited to offer poems for future volumes.

Postal enquiries should be accompanied by an SAE or the requisite number of international reply coupons. Please do not send poems by e-mail and please do not make general enquiries by telephone (unless already in dialogue with the editor).

This publishing venture is expressly non-profit-making; the revenue generated through book sales and the competition goes towards the costs of production, promotion and prizes.

The editor wishes to thank the University of Bristol English Department for help with postal expenditure and resources.

ISBN
0 9532981 3 2

ISSN
1462-5016

THE
TABLA
Book of New Verse

The Tabla Book of New Verse sets selected entries submitted to the *Tabla* poetry competition alongside work by former contributors and established authors. As in previous volumes, the order of contents here has been prompted by serendipitous connections between the poems. Thus, the reader will often see a particular word, idea or image in one poem lifting a latch on the next...

Thanks are due to the following for advice and 'Tabla talk': Helen Bolton, Peter Carpenter, Stephen Cheeke, Jess Dunton, Andrew Johnston, Sarah Law, Philip Lyons, Samantha Matthews, Steven Matthews, Philippa Nokes and Mark Willis. Thank you in particular to Anne Stevenson for judging last year's competition entries and for providing helpful feedback.

STEPHEN JAMES

Poems

Information

★*indicates 2000 competition entry*

Winners of the 2000 *Tabla* poetry competition

FIRST PRIZE   Henry Shukman, *Piano Solo*

SECOND PRIZE   Anne Berkeley, *Gasometer*

RUNNERS–UP   Julia Copus, *Regret*
Kathleen Jones, *Above Middleton*
M. R. Peacocke, *Snail*

SPECIAL COMMENDATIONS   Alison Brackenbury, *Blackthorn Winter*
Mario Petrucci, *Amaretti*
Mario Petrucci, *Sniper*

SELECTED BY   Anne Stevenson

A revised version of Anne Berkeley's
'Gasometer', differing slightly from the
version judged by Anne Stevenson, appears
in this volume with the latter's approval.

Piano Solo

Years after my mother chose emptiness
at night I'd hear her at the piano
planting chords, waiting for them
to grow into something.

She never advanced from childhood
lessons. She'd crackle flat a dry page
of Bartok or Anna Magdalena
and make the house's spine go cold.

That was all her hesitant handfuls
conjured – misery, a lonely beginner
always beginning again, a weather
of notes I wished would pass.

They trickled onto my sheets
in the dark, each drop telling
how sad a woman could feel
even to have lost what made her sad.

HENRY SHUKMAN

White Noise

Some say it's endless night,
no moon, no day,
but can you hear my working hands
tug weeds away?
Rosa-rugosa trowelled in
smells apple-sweet in rain.
You loved to sleep.
I rested in your shade.

Here cemetery men
in masks, with strimmers,
raise storms of grass
around these close-packed graves.
My broken nails,
embedded with your clay,
take nothing home...
You ride the water's tail
and twist away.

Some say it's white,
the tunnel's eye, perpetual light,
an Arctic summer's day.
Is God white noise
or does He sing
with indigo, Payne's grey?
The torture game is played
with endless light.

This is the field
forbidden to the angels
and Jesus hangs his head
behind those trees.
Sleep here in peace
the long sleep of the Jews
with that essential star
you lit for me.

JILL BAMBER

Edgar Alwin Payne (1882–1947): American
water-colourist, noted for his deep grey skies.

The Turbot
after Rilke, Sonnets to Orpheus, II, xx

From star to star, what emptiness extends!
Here on Earth, between our own lives, greater by far
the distances. Take that child, playing with friends.
How remote from each other even the closest are.

Our fate lies in ourselves, which makes it strange.
Into a silent future we propel our lives.
When a girl fails to meet you at the moated grange,
and hides her love, how alien her motives.

Everywhere distance, the circle incomplete.
The turbot, asymmetrically dead, attends our grace.
How weird its expression on the serving-dish!

Lifted to heaven, white eyes, in mute defeat,
withhold the sea's wisdom – that in a wilder place
we too might mouth inaudibly, like fish.

ROBERT SAXTON

Darwinian

An invasion mechanism: the fish sift the water.
They ingest the right particles, also the wrong.
Bacteria implode under the stomach's pressure.
Surviving microbes migrate to dorsal flesh.

Two freshwater biologists in a smack, upstream.
An hypothesis as thin as the paper they wrote it on.
Tears at bedtime for fish with the bacterium-strain.
Their eyes, pustular. Their considerations, air.

A boat, humped over, in the littoral of a river.
A beetle heading – where – across its bow.
Science at midnight on the far edge of a lake.
Our best work carried out on the shore of sleep.

The observations: tiny, as essential as daybreak:
a reedbed rowing its sundial out of sync;
a spider hauling dead up in rainbows;
and Saprolegnia, a parasite of fish.

I turned into a fish one morning and drowned.
Fish-hearted at The Benefit, I had lost my face.
How I swam into unemployment. How my girl's face knew.
In Parasite Science, no place for this knowledge.

The humane director of the freshwater laboratory.
He was 'released from employment' with one week's notice.
His final task was to sack all his staff.
I met him twice afterwards. We had lost our faces.

He lost himself in a gardener's job.
The Park's Department had a place for his knowledge.
Someone, somewhere has place for our knowledge.
The local park had the place for his knowledge.

Christ calls from the kitchen. We make lunch together.
Fish. Let's grill them, but we strip off their skin.
We flense off the parasites, wait for the five thousand.
Then I wrap him in white lines like a Bird Eating Spider.

DAVID MORLEY

14

Nibbling

Her favourite colour
is despotic weed.
Devastated cobwebs
cling to her lashes. She's

a crazed dictator, disappearing
whole families of scorching pink.
The pin faces of forget-me-nots
giggle disbelievingly as she opens wide.

She rips the hearts out of dandelions,
and snaps the backs of mint in two.
In dreams I carry her

tightly in my arms
and I set her gently down
wherever lawns have lost their mind.

POLLY CLARK

First Garden

Despite trays of lobelia, kilos
of shop-bought soil, the wildlife
gathers force. Cabbages gnawed,
bulbs stolen in a flurry of earth,
tell-tale slime up deflowered stems.

This soil is sour on my hands,
comforts and scares me, as I break
clay packed with crocks and bone,
search out the stark white roots
of bindweed. Arcs of bramble
dog the path. A city fox trails
down berry-stained concrete.

I spend evenings without light,
windows open, the garden growing
wilder, each shift of darkness
magnified by what I've seen
on midnight trips to water –

how a toad makes the garden jump
then waits, black-backed in the hebe,
how a snail, horns stirring, attends
the scented feeding grounds.

I wedge the gate, attempting
ownership with all the boundaries
reversed. A watchful passion
is worming in, the harvest unexpected.

KATHERINE PAGE

Clematis Petals

Clematis petals follow me in –
winged seeds, pollen and various dusts –
when I close the door for the night
on the copious garden;
                    behind me the house is inert,
the air unstirred, the surfaces untouched.
The house can't be inhabited enough
                    for that lived-in look
the garden doesn't need.

I close the door reluctantly
on the massing dark of the trees.
They open their arms
to welcome me into a night in the forest
to sleep amidst its intense activities.

It was another kind of life
in the rare air of glass high-rises
beyond the reach of roving seeds, stray flies,
the darkness never quite arriving –
the life I couldn't lead.

This time, this hour,
this doorway is a cusp
where even now I don't quite dwell.
The seasons should dissolve
into one another as the sift of May
drifts in. But they collide here.
May is erupting
into the autumn of the house –
the hermitage of its rooms –
dark curtains, the peace of long winter.

JUDY GAHAGAN

Cornflower

You come upon me in a field.
I am sky looking up to sky
so you wonder where your opposites
have gone. You pitch between sleep
and waking, tell the dream
it is not. But I am what you know,
remember? The colour of every best shirt,
your valiant ink finger, your sunk-
in-the-glass memory. I survive.
The sun may burn me out
to wide blue, lost blue, to blue faded through
to white at the edges.
But there is blue in the evening
burning softly in the gloom,
in an ordinary kitchen where I leave no scent.
I stand easy in the jug.
I am there in your hands.
No need to proclaim me – I am no noisy
orange flower in a hood of cellophane.
I speak your language, leave sap
on your fingers, across your sheet of paper.
Look at my gathering of petals –
how could they be closer?
My sooty black heart –
how could it not say what it feels?

ROBERT SEATTER

The Lady's Mantle Letter

She will write him a letter to tell him
  how cool and wet her garden is this July,
    how beautiful the alchemilla is,
      a strange citrus, petal-less froth above
        the green nearly-circles of the fanned leaves.

They are the shape of its other name –
  Lady's Mantle – an outspread cloak, pleats
    stitched with pearls of dew, scallop-edged;
      designed for wrapping and unwrapping,
        a honey-scented aphrodisiac.

Alchemilla is after alchemy –
  the magic water it breathes through its leaves
    part of the ancient recipe for melting
      metals into gold. She will tell him
        what waiting is and what it isn't.

She will write him a letter to tell him
  these things because she's feeling inside out
    and he's not there to unwrap her, wrap her
      in his pashmina arms; and because
        it's him she's thinking about when, by chance,

she places three stems of purple crane's bill
  in the same vase and catches the shock
    of both flowers growing more alive,
      their colours spilling into something new.
        She will tell him how soft the rain is.

LINDA FRANCE

Hurricane Edge
New York 1999

A leaf bobbed like a float.
First stipple on dusty slabs. Peck
on the cheek, the childish kiss
of rain. Kiss the shining rods of rain.
The lish beat filled. A canvas sky,
slung between buildings, darkened, sagged,
came suddenly unsheeted.

Some ran. Some, what could we do
but stand in the downdrag, thinned,
punched through like zinc?
Hair smeared to the scalp
like trodden grass, we gazed
at the eelback thresh of gutters,
tranced to the bone with rain.

A yellow pickup
hacked into water, shoaled it
rim over rim in blowsy fans,
rode through on throbbing din, got out –
just – on the swash, left us
blasted, heads wide open
like dynamited fish,

shocked into knowing that rain
could build to a bulging cornice
and it would happen: scribbled cracks
in plaster mouthing open, trees
and houses gaping and losing grip,
rampage of sullen water,
cries under the wind.

And now the city's dazed,
still gingerly balanced, footfast
in pulpy ground, up to its pulse
in trash; but we can walk
on a willowpattern sky, threading
the squares and streets together,
putting the horizons back.

We've found our rhythm, dryshod
passacaglia, ordinary present.
We could go shopping. Only
we've seen the news, the paper's here
with photos of cockeyed roofs, woods
broomed down, sprawling cars, a logjam
in North Carolina of drowned sows.

We've read some names. Yet we're baptised,
for reasons we can't fathom,
into belief in safety, sitting
on the right hand of luck, able
for now to tell our nearly tales,
reprieved; while a fist in a pocket
stays closed on a sprig of guilt.

M. R. PEACOCKE

Regret

There could be a monster, madman or harpy
in that hard-shelled seed you buried recently,

thinking *It is limbless what harm can possibly
come of it?* Alone now in the soft-soiled grainy

dark, it's using all its balled-up energy
to split the husk, push out a tiny gristly

root ... Oh, you can't hear it but already
it's making headway, nudging a pasty-

looking stem towards the light, sensing a carefully
shaped hole for it to bloom into, surgically

cut for it out of the indigo sky. What a panoply
of stories it will tell when it bristles with willowy

arms and legs of its own! Yes, it is undeniably
out of your hands. Look at it logically:

the split seed-coat can't be resealed. It's crazy
to think you might undo the harm, sew up the squally

storm inside its clouds. All the same it's best to be wary –
for days, months, years later when your dinner-party

guests are stepping inside from the shiny
moonlight-lacquered pavements of whatever city

you are living in, when the wine is quietly
breathing in its jug, the silver-plated cutlery

is silent and anxious, going over its clattery
small-talk on the polished table, then your heavy-

hearted monster will lean its bulk over your chimney-
stack and, with a kind of funnelled clarity,

attestations to your cruelty, words of such enormity
will issue, issue, issue from its mouth.

JULIA COPUS

Vivaldi's Mistress

He carries music in his breath
from the vestry to her door,
still hearing damp drip
on altar gold, candles stutter
the shapes that he must make.

Cold sharpens his face, his fingers
numb from bracing chords.
Doctors tell him not to breathe
night-mists from the lagoon,
to grease his chest and bleed.

This city always draws him back.
A black prow peels the water,
sends fat slaps washing to his feet –
the sounds that he was born to
worn through the steps and piers.

He must slow the movement.
Drone bass as an undertow,
lead mutes on the drowsy strings,
lower G rising, insistent
as a face blanched in the water.

He taps their code out,
lets water-light move walls
muffled in gilt and brocade.
And where she waits in silence,
he gives his beloved sleep.

KATHERINE PAGE

The Room of the Model Theatre Sets
for Sebastiano Romano

The end of the century. In your flat
Mimi is still dying again and again, Tosca mounting
the crenellated battlements.

            Your Sicilian *pupi*
are dangling on the wall, the curl of their moustaches
liquorice-black, their mouths' bright lipstick

unsmudged by kisses. And of course the arrows,
drooping so elegant from your Saint Sebastian's flesh –
the little statue decorous under the lamplight –
white as a peach and beautiful, I remember,

so beautiful in the dark. In your designer's model theatre sets
all the paper cut-outs tremble on their sticks,
wave their tiny hands up to the light. You wake

with a start from your long insomnia, show me
the photos of the dead and dying: the razor blade cuts
that sting in the morning, the weight that makes
no space at all. You shout about graffiti on the Milan streets,

all along the train carriages unmoving in their tracks,
the sound of aerosol cans night after night –
            illegible smears in the unlovely morning.

ROBERT SEATTER

Celeste

The morning I was born, my father was milking
Celeste, leaning in against her warm flank,
jersey onion skin yellow, unravelling at the elbow.

My mother was painting my birth,
my brother's death; his body the shape of a cross
above us, my face a flower bursting from her.

Beneath her dress stitched from a brocade curtain,
I emerged as my father carried in a pail of goat's milk.
But nowhere is the kingfisher, that clot of blue,

that beat its wings against the wall,
as the baby tangled his fingers
in my mother's hair and screamed.

In the painting my brother's thumbs
curl inwards in agony, his fingers long as the bullrushes
my father waded through roadside swamps for.

My mother would arrange them on a claw-footed table
gramophone under the window, blown eggs
on crimson cords hung above the doors.

I remember the piquancy of the guava berries,
and how my mother let me milk her into Agee jars.
After the birth of Celeste's three kids the house

filled with bleats, the tap of hooves as they ran
down the hall. They should have been weaned
but no one had the heart and all of us suckled on.

The night Celeste died there was a heavy dew.
She cried to come inside, but even a roaring fire
could not stop her shivering. I woke, saw my father

kneeling by the grate, her head cradled in his hand.
A deep tremor started in her ear, travelled through her body.
No bird came but the trees beat against the glass.

PAOLA BILBROUGH

The Dream Hotel

As if the sea were entering through the window,
it was that close. Flecks of burning ice thrown
from the rocks it struck, each single fleck blown
sharp-toothed into the house. Meanwhile, below
there were guests waiting to check in, a clerk
to register them, luggage piling at doors.
This was the form of the dream. Polished floors
were swimming in water, a green-grey dark.
From the top of the cliff you could see rain
gathering on the horizon, not yet ready
to fall but on its way. In one room two lips
were joined together, hands resting on hips,
the pair of them increasingly unsteady
as the flood rolled in like an enormous stain.

You wake to a light on the ceiling. How long
have you been awake? You lie next to him,
the one you always lie with. Some vague, dim
recollection. Years of memory. The song
of the sirens. The glow of the clock-radio
is green and gentle. Classical music, faint,
barely audible, oozes from it. Something quaint
about all this, your life passing on its slow
unforgiving way. The shape in the bed stirs
in its sleep, rolls over. You feel the steady swell
rising in you. You hear the sea again.
It is still far off, a slowly approaching train
down a long tunnel that leads to the hotel
and the two lovers, just as his lips touch hers.

GEORGE SZIRTES

27

Journey

Each fist beat of this train is distinct,
the lub-dup hammer clear at full speed.

It's dark: through the window suburban lights
are numerous and dull as spiders' eyes.

The intercom hisses but no-one speaks.
I think of our legs cleaving

with the stuck delicacy of crane flies,
then suck in a little air to inflate

my lungs, still crushed from the weight
of your chest. I'm punch-drunk,

weathering the square-cornered swings
of a ghost-train. I'm coffined

in this rust-pinned torso
passing the black bridge topped

with brambles of black cast iron,
jutting up to a sky pinkish

with breath and exhaust.
I fight into sleep, head

jolted against the smeared window
and picture myself under you again,

each muscle tacked down like a cable
unable to move. We swing into the station

with the carelessness of a missed step.
I wake to remember the ending,

the inside of me contracting
with the beating of wings.

SALLY READ

In This Instant

The tern's slow strokes against the wind palping it
before the pause the drop the vanishing. Or to be
on the go always, headlong heartstrong heartwhole
like the sandmartin in the behind-the-wind silence
of the cliff-face, the sound of it matching the clicking
of two stones in your pocket while the lark cries out
on high, wired to its spot and going musically mad
before the stop the drop the silence, then the greeting
the sandmartin gets at the pueblo opening as she
slows hovers stops to enter and no grain disturbed
while a single pink of thrift shakes its desiccate head
shivering, and near the road the bee deals with
the buttercup, the buttercup with the bee, and every
thing is buzz and tremble till an instant's stillness,
insidedness, you feel the give and take of it, all the
rhyme reason speechless recognition of it, and proceed.

EAMON GRENNAN

Redemption

Air-conditioning shivers your arms
as you drive the bend
into Badlands –
        scorched air faltering
over clay, sand, volcanic ash:
you could be looking through
an oven door.

The slender peaks
are wind – water sculptures,
geologists say.

But the geometry
of its dark pink markings
is inexhaustible,
an army of layers;
        the insane pink rings of a snake.

If you flew a small plane
you might see a dozen black dots
lost between knuckles of rock:
        suicides stepped off into wilderness;
oubliettes where each turn muffles
in soft ash,
soaking up sound like water.

As you pose for that photo, perched
with your back to reptilian pink,
        your shadow thinned to a knife-edge,
hot wind is absorbing your breath
and your face is white with sweat.

You can't know
how you'll drive the loop
through tangles of coneflowers,
the dark scrutiny of Lakota,

till you come to a cemetery
fenced off on a black-scrub hill.
The way each plot is anchored
                    with crystals, pebbles, dried corn
                    and chokecherries;

the steady rot of berries,
stones, weighing down souls.

And a dreamcatcher
hung on one headstone, filtering
grit,
sustained dreams.
                    As if thoughts give off from the dead
                    like that final growth of hair;
                    a quiet precipitation.

SALLY READ

Heroic

Everything on the edge of the drop,
and I, as if already falling,
decapitate you in these old photographs in Ronda.

Inside the hotel we ate game. A long meal
under high ceilings. Linen shrouded
tables laid with heavy knives.

The bar roared in the late afternoon as we
surfaced blinking into a hot crowd of red
and gold, gathering for the corrida

and, at the centre of the noise, a woman
like a doll or a bird, gallant
in the capework of her glance.

Back at the house holding onto pink rocks,
my head was full of fire. I lived in fear
of flames and dared not smoke.

On the front page of the paper, Gorbachev's
naked face on a screen in his dacha
where he wore his Tolstoyan shirt stared

into the unthinkable. The radio
crackled its news in the dark. On every side
the night animals pressed

their advantage while we sweated it out
on the edge of the drop, by the light of the moon, about
to surrender to ritual, to insert the sword.

LEONIE RUSHFORTH

Army Sewing Kit

I had never seen him sew in my life.
Not a button. Not a hem.

Now here was this tiny package – and him telling me
how every man had been taught to use it.

Six round buttons in three different sizes,
tough khaki twine, red and white cotton thread
around a cardboard band, four pins
and a single gold-tipped needle.

His large square fingers became suddenly deft,
pulled the twine against the light,
through the needle, through one spinning button,
then down flat against the cloth.

And suddenly he was sewing for his life.
He had no son, no room to clear, no house
to move. There was just this moment.

Then the next. The silence and the terrible noise
inside the silence. Then the button anchored
tight at the edge of the collar. I could see it

right against his Adam's apple, and him
swallowing hard again and then again.

ROBERT SEATTER

33

The Trout at Istok

Past Rakos again, dusk descending:
Two horses, statuesque, stilled in a meadow:
Sandbags of the Spanish base camouflaged

Next to the torched skeletons of cabs and tankers,
A ribwork of girders,
All awash in swift rust: that burnt white Zastava

Run aground at the frozen yield of a junction,
Mottled and ash-wealed, still ghosting
The death-ride's forking to the big site in the pines

Like the metempsychosis of a terrible time
Fleeing the flash-fireball of its moment:
Prairie dusk, descending

The bend by the sign, I motioned
The driver to stop. Exactly what was
I hoping for, standing

Here again? What loss already? Between Pec and Istok
Under purplish Montana-gaze
Of the Accursed Mountains, we had turned back

To Pristina. Whatever it was, it was after
The hour in Istok; when I leant over the wavering weir
That moated the restaurant's octagonal isle

Myriads of dark trout rose and flickered
To my peering shadow
As if a flock of swifts flicking its being

To a charm of glimmers. Beer and linen had brought us
Back from the dead; but now, moving off
Towards the taxi, two teenagers materialized

To bring us back to two-hours-back. Gestures. What?
Afrim? Not Afrim? What, then? Spine? Skull?
A girl? Yes. Unidentified...? Of course. Yesterday

The Australian from the Tribunal:
We are not a body removal operation
If the evidence is immaterial. Little orphan corpse,

Resurrected in memory, excuse me the nod
That fetched their shovel down the road,
That let them scrape at the shallow clods

And lift a binbag hem from the tresses at your nape,
That gave me to shift just a jot
The black plastic shrouding the hollow of your ribs,

Then for the longest of seconds to look upon
The monkey-grimace of your baby teeth
In the O of their parchment mask;

Though, later,
The voice of truth would whisper
As our car passed a boy with a whittled wooden pitchfork,

The moon hung high and pure and full
Over gloaming's prairieland lit by wildfires: confront it
As one would any other, that thing you have become forever.

CHRIS AGEE

Afrim: Albanian for Abraham

Przewalski's Horse

Out of Tachijn-Shar-Nuru, the land surveyor –
a Polish-Russian, appointed by the Czar –
surveyed his unlikely prize:
                    a skull and hide
Kirghizian hunters claimed belonged to *takhi*,
spirit of the Yellow Mountains, untamed
cousin of his own cinched and harnessed
stallion agraze outside the tent.
                             A wild horse
this late in the day?
                    He doubted, but attended
as the horsemen (fur-decked, rail-boned,
untranslated) spoke of rampant herds
ghosting across the steppe, invisible
but audible, distant clouds of hooves
dismissing history, swift as windstorms,
disturbing only grass and stone.
                         Near impossible
to bring to ground, outpacing sprung arrows,
wildering pursuers past limits
                        (their hollowed eyes,
staring through like rents in old maps,
gaping landscapes)
                  but not at last
the civil bullet
                whistling some to dead halts,
encrypted posings,
                  bodies gathered and fenced
in the horizon's wide pen.

He studied the remnant hefted in his hands –
live token of bone and integument,
like confirmation of the life to come –
to puzzle out its story:
                                        residue of spirit
ancient evolution
                                akin at last to nothing
but steppe and wind
                                riderless vehicle
(flat-backed, stiff-maned)
                                        scripting the plain
in the complicated texture
                                        of his own inherited name.

DAVID GRAVENDER

Sniper
4 February 1944

With him, it's personal.
I've seen him gape clear through
an eggshell skull. That shuddering
finish. A sally's different:

death, then, a uniform affair.
But in his sights the cock
of a hat, a quirk of hair, and
that's it. This thread, not that,

snagged from the future.
They caught one once – confessed
he would track his mark a full watch,
get to know them real well

before the shot resolved itself.
Another would wait till you
were taking tea with your mates,
then drop you in full view.

When you hear things like that
your back plays cat's cradle
with its tendons, trying to get you real
small. Christ – to be a tot again,

tucked between blankets of rock.
He's out there right now. At dawn
clipped a toe clean off the corporal's boot.
Scrunched his face black as croup.

Last week he was drilling insignias.
Two officers, for a lark, took
to restitching them on their arse.
That's the thing about war – adapt.

No point going stark-staring
working out the chances. Some
have a sense – stall a fraction
before his finger squeezes –

his cross-hairs tickle
their nape. Most get caught
pants round ankles. Me, I'm
ready. Inside, already dead.

Sure, I keep my head down.
But your guts know the next nook
could fetch you smack up against it.
That sudden relaxation. The forever look.

MARIO PETRUCCI

Taking Leave
In memory of Patrick Hayman

Flat-footed, exempt from war,
he sailed through the Suez, and felt
an unfurling, a stretching towards light,
as though a rusty-headed fern grew inside.

Crossing the dateline, he forgot
to be meticulous; wore a crumpled shirt,
let salt crust his skin. Arriving,
I would like to think, he drank tea,

amber in the glass, a sugar cube between his teeth.
I'd like to think that his relatives wore
yamulkes and side locks. But they'd long
since taken leave of religion and Europe.

Tea, cloudy with milk, was served
in thick railway china. His cousin's hands
were furious with nerves; incessantly
scribbling lines of verse or smoothing

silk handkerchiefs that rose,
pale tulips, from his breast pocket.
A man more comfortable in motion;
knapsack on back, tweed trousers rolled up,

paper and ink in case an idea struck.
In photographs the poet-cousin looks austere.
And Patrick, a man with small padded hands,
sleepy eyes turned down at the corners.

Moving north, he conceived my mother
with another's wife. But didn't stay.
Eleven years away, he returned to England
with a country behind his lids; wind-frayed trees,

long pale coasts ready to unroll into paintings.
In the foreground a plane with his own bearded face
and sometimes a rabbi striding in a tall hat.
Pieces of self, airborne, unfettered by location.

PAOLA BILBROUGH

Out of Place

Backs of lorries turn respectable;
a madness begins in queues.
Automatic weapons look coy
in the arms of strangers.

The opposite is true. The opposite
to what you have always known –
no streetnames, no burials,
and only the clothes you stand up in.

Houses are pocked and eaten.
A woman in a headscarf returns
with flowers, and she is bitter,
bitter as small grapefruit.

You salvage what you can
from the weak and dying,
but you are still marginalia,
errata, part of the problem.

It first hit you on a country road:
the woods turned to camouflage,
and lovers were on the run from
sweethearts combing the long grass.

HOWARD WRIGHT

Caste

"In the out-of-season park
where the mossed toilets are padlocked,
where the trees throw their leaves –
the dead leaves that rush the bowling green, the tennis court
in their wild packs and drifting onlys –
is where we sometimes meet the best
in our secret England,
at least two towns out of our Indian homes
where she slips the bobby pins
from the black following hair
and sits alongside me
on the bench of white people's graffiti
where we put from mind the feud we just might begin
and as we turn our backs on the owed life
she sometimes starts to lose herself
and gets over-close with me, gets my palm,
eyes wider than the dare of her love, she looks outward
through the toxic light that blanks her face,
through the wood and the iron fences
and stares on to the Uxbridge Road, she stares for miles,
she stares for all the traffic lights to merge green,
she tells me how she would really like to live
on the quick road from there to the M4,
to keep going with me
as far as we need to
until we are past conviction, past ourselves and hidden."

KHAN SINGH KUMAR

Wedding Nerves
from 'Oubliette'

It is night in the town, peeling paint dark
where a line of punts lies tethered, nosing
at the boathouse wall. Close by here a man,
who isn't yet my father, is hinging
his footfalls to the river-path with endless
pacing – heel to toe, and on and back,
each turning point a god's hand gathering
the yarn of his distracted mind.
Tall branches shape a larynx for the wind.
My father has no voice tonight, but look –
his hair is lit like words as if the moon
has lifted it the way it lifts the river
to coax a secret language from the water.
The world is shifting imperceptibly,
he seems to say, and if I add to this,
if I add – click, click – the speed of my steps,
how fast, then, am I moving and how soon
will it be morning...
                              And now he stops, mid-
thought, mid-path, remembering the cold
holiness of that winter church, the banns
read out and how he flushed and felt the growth
that itches from a root in early spring
and blazes in the bud and anything
seemed possible, in reach, and was, as if
he had been brought out of the womb again
where no eye had seen him.
                              Tomorrow
he will be husband like the tallest tree.

JULIA COPUS

44

Side-Effects

"...wake now or never
    For if thou nodd'st thou fall'st, and falling, fall forever."
                        FRANCIS QUARLES, *Emblems* (1635)

That morning you were lying-in, stirring sometimes
in the turbulence of an overcast, late-April heat,
dreaming of entering a pharmacy, drinking a cup of methadone
then rocking a lion to sleep in your arms
while stroking its mane in an olive-grove.
It's the anti-depressants, you start to explain that night,
they leave me so lethargic I can barely move...
You are weighing Serge Gainsbourg & Brigitte Bardot
against Stereolab's *Refried Ectoplasm,*
Bonnie & Clyde against *Harmonium,*
seeking something, anything, that might lift the mood.
It's so hard, you say, *to want to be awake*
when there's only work, this room and debt to be conscious in...
You press POWER and PLAY, then set REPEAT.
I'm alright really, just a bit run down.
Tell me a story. Keep me entertained.
There's a joke about penguins you've heard before,
a 'twenties cocktail called an *'Angel's Tit'.*
You turn away, stare out over rooftops, yards, yet listen hard,
follow the thoughts that slip unvoiced
behind the words I use. *It was strictly two-thirds cherry liqueur,*
one-third cream with a cherry on top.
You'd drink it and think you'd seen the face of God.
Buttercups nod on a darkening lawn
and ivy slumps like a safety-net
in the shadows thrown by a carriage-lamp.
You tell me you're watching your own mind work from a long way off,
does that make sense, or are you going mad?
The orange upglare of the skyline burns
like rushlight on armoured, unmoving cloud.

WAYNE BURROWS

The Gods of Tiepolo

1.

Sometimes when you look up on a bright day,
the clouds have drawn apart, exposing a blue
that, for a moment, you can almost look through.
You're surveying a stage long after the play
has finished. Above you, Tiepolo
presents a weightless mass of gods and legs
in endless apotheosis, delicate as eggs
in a cup, or naked skin in an afterglow
when legs and arms float off into half-sleep
and breasts settle warmly against the ribcage
slipping vaguely down its slopes, while the flat
lower belly shimmers and fingers keep
curling and uncurling like an open page
in a slight breeze. But you can imagine that.

2.

So you imagine it – although this is
the soft sell version, somewhere beyond which
the world is singing at a sharper pitch,
its shrieks full of glass, crowded with casualties:
men in ridiculous wigs, women with waists
pinched to a tight ring, thin children in beds
with soiled sheets, the poor with their shaved heads
and hollow eyes, cruel sexual gymnasts
one step from madness, new forms of rough trade,
a puritan hell which no amount of light
can keep from sinking deeper into flames.
Imagine it. And through that? The betrayed
clear blue of something very simple, as trite
as touch, the sound of the most common names.

3.

You listen to them. It's no different there
next door, next year. The sky is lightly cracking.
An enormous gentleness billows its wing
and you too are up aloft, somewhere in the air
on an internal flight, your safety belt
clipped shut, with a glass of whisky on the rocks
on a swivelling tray, among lazy flocks
of clouds that snuggle up to you then melt,
substantial as any god or human life.
Now you're a god. There's something piercing and sad
about this knowledge, as if there were nothing but
that rococo blue which beggars all belief,
the world below disordered, a ragged, mad
arena of blood which runs and refuses to clot.

4.

In this particular Tiepolo,
The Finding of Moses, where a Venetian
beauty, dressed in the height of contemporary fashion,
stands in for the daughter of the Pharaoh,
your eyes discover a female figure, vast
thighed yet slender and long, with cheekbones sleek
as a greyhound and eyes that plead to speak
a mind so powerful it makes your own fly fast.
The even blue sky above her seems to spring
straight from her gaze which comprehends your own.
It solves the world, bandages its wounds,
ties up its severed limbs with blood-soaked string,
walks the streets of explosions up and down,
and smiles at all its terrible, sad sounds.

5.

Keep flying, pilot, We're gods of air and fire,
our clay feet stuck in loam. Bring me a drink
and let me watch the clouds move as I think
of something clear as glass in the empire
of the bladed, whose agents are generous.
I'm fed up of this Rococo court, that sits
tremendous-arsed, and will shortly be blown to bits
on its mountain-top five-star hotel terrace.
It's dark outside. Soon the movies come on
with hollow icons and interminable chases.
I want a woman of luminous intelligence to heal
my hypochondria. Soon we shall land on the sun
with smooth, unruffled, tanned, innocent faces,
staring at endless blue. It's no big deal.

GEORGE SZIRTES

Muybridge's Room

And so this brute and sweating space
gathers shadows, the printed shapes
of animals, then naked men and women,
their bodies dumpy in the fashion of their time,
the beige and pink parabolas of buttocks,
the swell of thighs measured, the empire's muscles.

What remains is photography
and, jumping through, come tricks of vision,
pictures of life and verity,
a circus of the real, stripped bare of costume,
free of colour and bangle and shimmer,
the better to see the truth, make things clear.

In black and white, arms and legs, how she bends,
again picks up a flower, rises, takes two steps...

But in his mind it is different;
here each flash reveals her, spotlights
her, for a second, flaring for a minute,
or the ends of hours. The sequence,
always unfinished, glimmers on
the edge of chronology, always partial;

white shape against blue, voice and sparkle
blooming against the sound of the clock
for years after she has gone. Then at last, when

he becomes clear, he sees the space in his mind
empty as a pit and remains there for days,
staring into all the desolation of it.

IAN STARSMORE

Palmer Exhibition

Eagle and lamb are equal in his eyes
and bats in the distance, a hair-line caught,
a moon often above some heavy trees,
a tower without question in the hills,
and always the threat that angels appear.

This view passes with a change in autumn,
a yoke of oxen almost going slow:
women muscle with baskets on their heads,
and now the valley is stretched like jewels
held to the light as if it lives again.

Not many here, dark so they will not fade,
with stops by countryside no longer wild,
but it looks like a never-ending heather
and the signs are still thought a place for thieves
or what is a midday affair, all smiles.

At every pause which follows we are lost
in stacked-up corn, the golden detailed air
just out of grasp and one or two sunsets
building over the path we used to take,
leaving us bones and some bewildered fields.

They come and go not sure if they are flames
or signify the blossom of a night,
touching some lips as if to make a point,
and then wake up in woods and see the sky
as a frame or a gap, never the time.

LAWRENCE BRADY

Amateur Photography

They're useless as evidence – you can hardly see
anything but colours. And how the colours blur – no edges,
only a gradual shift
from mostly green to mostly brown,
yet the precise thing I was interested in
was edge, the spider over the edge
in air defined by edges the sculptor chose.

'Clean lines' – there's little by way of gesture or frill:
massive, blocky, the sort of girl
you wouldn't want to cross. She occupies
the top end of the garden under the chestnuts
with her back to the lawn,
not caring for the view.
Her lightly closed fist could hold a spray of chestnut candles.

Every morning you touch her necklace.
I try to guess where. There's no trace
of your finger on the sharp ridge
over her collarbone, or the soft fold
where lichen has gathered, ochre and lime.

I'm trying to record four dimensions in two:
the surface, and the space
above the surface where your hand might have paused.
The spider glues her anchor-holds in lichen
and when she launches herself
into the wind and light
she's overexposed but you can just see her
running upside down, two toes at a time
on her own thread. She will catch
the gorgeous blue fly
basking like a jewel on the shoulder.

ANNE BERKELEY

Ephemeroptera
for Amy Miner

It will have no stomach,
no mouth

and live for one day.
Baby mayfly

I almost pinched
in hot fingers

like a gnat, a midge,
though yellow as butter,

and new-hatched legs
wobbly as a calf's.

But a mouth that can't
suckle,

or mold flapping
questions

round a tongue.
And a body with no stomach

can't sense hunger
streaming up;

can't fester on masses
of luminous thoughts

that would nest there
like cod's roe.

No, these confettis are sealed
in their destinies,

blindfolded,
tongueless geisha

in their yellow kimonos,
sliding

over non-existent
ripples of air,

before shedding wings,
spraying eggs

in a wedding dance.
The coup de grace:

submitting
in one black skin

on the belly
of the bronze

late-summer lake
to a glut of trout.

And gifted
in this vanishing

as though lost
between loud heads

in a crowd; absorbed
painlessly

into a snow-fall
of light;

imperceptible
as cobwebs strung

over trees, sticky
and strong.

SALLY READ

Butterfly, Breath, Small Birds

Butterfly in tar: a stained-glass fossil.
And this laurel tree, green all winter –
ramifying, dreaming households.
Heart-ice, cloudlight, geese floating over:
whose future in their feathered bones?
Bloodbeat and heart-thump steady as they go.

Breasts and everything on show,
but it's the pierced right ear
he finds his eye going back to: room so cold
they could see their breath at bloodheat
frosting the windowpane,
blinding its clear unlying eye.

Two small birds in the leafless ginko:
through steelblue chill their pure
antiphonal whistling. Then a sudden
shuddering warmth: his jacket, her arms
around it. He's inside somewhere, feeling
each button, knuckle, lips that tilt away.

Such sharp song they had, and clean green throats.

EAMON GRENNAN

Snail

Snail pearls footlucid from the infant cluster,
eases to a vegetable deep, mouthing
his trawl, his greenlit mumble.

Unfurls a muscle of his foraging eye
and coasts like a swan in shadow,
mushing his meat of leaves.

Once, painted my spread palm with his
on an upward slicksilver piste, and showed me
how the world hangs and pulses;

and will disc himself in, cellar his kiss
all winter, build his occlusions
like the bowl of a fine horn spoon.

M. R. PEACOCKE

Bowl

Handturned, so light, it carries
the fragrance of redgum.
Winter in Yarralumla, the lawn
strewn with pieces of bark
the trees have stepped out of.
Rosellas have flown from Astrolabe
and the children at the Ecole Maternelle
wear mittens now, hurry into cars.

The aboriginal ambassador,
at his desk outside the caravan,
counts coins in a bowl.
Black hands and footprints
trample over its roof and walls,
searching. Inside the portrait gallery
his manacled ancestors
refuse to meet your eye.

CAROLE BROMLEY

Owl-Glass

The first time, the eye spies a spy-glass:
owl-glass
a till-now-unheard word:

thick spectacles, a monocle, binoculars
to track nocturnal birds?
Or a barometer that measures owl-weather?
Dusky, silt-blue, cool,
without night the feel of night,
the time Minerva's owl is said to fly...

Yet no: godwit crossed with cuckoo,
owl-glass flies from Germany,
Eulenspiegel,
it darts, it does turns, it twits you:
jester, trickster,
it smiles and beams an image of the reader back
who stares, dumb-struck, wide-eyed, foolishly.

And yet the mind insists:
it is a word through which it still will bird-watch.
Barn. Barred. Great Horned. Great Grey.
Eastern Screech. Eagle Eyes. Snowy. Morepork.

Startled on thought's highbeam headlamp,
the heads swivel; large facial disks
channel sound into exceptional ears.
(Try to owl-prowl in the dark, in a nylon jacket:
how you'll wish for feather silencers
as your breath crackles static.)

Now the birds lift tented wings
their silhouettes beat higher on a slope of air,
thrum invisible drum skin;
the heart's suddenly audible palpitations.
Did you hear it, catch it?
Here. Try this. Owl-glass.

EMMA NEALE

Saxon Slave Clock

By ear instead of eye,
the time can be found in the dark,
the hour marks and hour lines
countersunk in the wheel.

A shadow falling on a flight of steps
in the neighbourhood of noon
is not perfectly sharp,
though walls flare and toss,

and the odd window of thin horn
burns with selected colour.
At a pre-set hour,
a self-going clock, being wound,

releases a light arm
carrying a jewel
on plain, uncut brass,
a pierced ruby as a bearing

distributing the new, marine hours
for the position of a ship at sea.
On the shortest winter afternoons,
or the shortest mornings,

the hands of clocks exposed
to the free wind and high weather,
count the light
of the mean, imaginary sun

like an ink trace
on a smoke surface,
quarter-chiming its celestial
equator, or the age of the moon.

At the outer end of spring,
the arc of their swing,
that was equal to the hours
during the major part

and near the mid-point
of the order of the day,
dies away closely.
It's the watchman's tell-

tale clock, driven inwards
by the four tides of a given star,
that's the ideal timekeeper,
night dial in a wood lantern.

MEDBH MCGUCKIAN

6, Sloop Lane

In a night air thick with low tide
and shadows of long-ago children
I trace that holiday-let among blind
alleys stepped up from the harbour.

I want you to know that the house
is smaller than I remember
an ill-fitted screen door and withered
Chronicles, a flat tube of glue
among flies on a teak windowshelf.

Promenade hotels echo to too few residents.

But you'd still know the out-of-hours dentist's
close by on the hill where I fretted with an abscess,
the gent's outfitters where we found
the stormcoat that never quite fitted.

I want to tell you every last
tang-laden, mast-clinking bit of it
but even if I could mail you
or waken the dead call-collect
you'd want to know what
in this world I was talking about.

ANNE–MARIE FYFE

House

It is the bleakest part of the shoreline,
Where brush huddles and wind snaps the flag poles.
After thirteen years and in autumn rain,
I stop, hear memory beat like a pulse.
But the house is sold, it says on the sign,
And I am on the road to somewhere else.

There were deaths and strange movements of money,
Letters from a member of parliament;
Hot days for flowers when there were any,
Long winters when the lights went out. And want
Meant have for a man whose past seemed shiny
But whose future would not leave the present.

I moved on and when they answered the door,
Someone else offered his card. Yet I think
Of all the afternoons between, the air
That passed along the window sill and sink,
Light flicking a plastic Eiffel Tower;
The smell, for all their polish, that stayed dank.

Now they have gone and I have appointments
Though there was love here of a sort that failed.
There was hope too, though for the wrong things, once,
And welcome, though the kettle never boiled.
And seawards I found, weed strewn by the fence,
Softly rotting roots whose trees had been felled.

IAN CAWS

Over Long Island

A swept rock garden. With an enormous rake
The lines of pebbles – roofs – have been made clear:
Their parallels leave rivulets, and bare
Calm soil along one edge, the Sound. Severe,
Like any rock garden in winter; so try to make

Its scale, its thumbprint creeks and springtail lakes
Bespeak
Not how smooth stones or snowflakes look alike
But what they thought they found when they came here:
Clean sidewalks. "Freedom from want. Freedom from fear."

STEPHEN BURT

Interstate 93

For a pure product of America,
                    for the optative continent,
Its vacant beauties, its unravelling vastness like cloud-processions
Drifting over the rim of the horizon,
                    take, for instance, Interstate 93
On a blue midsummer's evening, light rinsed and deepening,
North of Boston, north of Concord,
                    into the White Mountains;

The white in question
                    the birch that ghost the Indian green.
For a moment, you might think yourself
                    into a stretch of Russia.
Somewhere the highway will lie below you
Like beige sail-canvas threading the roiling wilderness;
Crossed perhaps by the Pemigewassett,
                    its brown bends

Like an insect's wing mirroring the sky's mother-of-pearl;
Its river stones and riffles
                    blanched and radiant as eye-markings...

CHRIS AGEE

Paper Birches

It will be night, or the hour before night,
and I'll be driving, shut-mouthed, alone,
down an unspooling county road,
tired eyes wandering, fingering
absently the ribbed bound spines
arrayed beyond scrubby verges,
tall volumes of spruce and alder,
massed codices of fir and cedar,
heavy-headed knowledge, nodding.
They'll glimmer out unexpectedly,
the birches, singly or in threes,
white moths dusting the twilight,
glimpsed whitenesses, visited
through open windows, side mirrors,
at fenced bounds of farms and fields,
milky presences as if assembling,
lank and pale, rich hair silvering
in late summer breezes, shimmering,
glossy as blank sheets on a desk
spangled with slanting light.

Small graces too brief to stare at,
elusive, nameless, more than common,
they are lonely not unbeautiful women,
bright-eyed, moon-faced. I'll recollect
some who taught me, tall ladies,
shawled or kerchiefed, long-fingered, with
so much to offer, their arts
and sciences, their deft explainings,
who'd disappear in the margins
of their pencilled annotations.

The forest's diarists, their voices
come as the riffling of onionskin.
They whisper names, and numbers,
angles of trajectory, points of view,
scales, modes, changes of key;
the knowledge that the world is a world
of appearance, and disappearance,
a finespun skin of in-betweenness,
an unscrolling palimpsest,
a commonplace book of my own making,
a fingering chart of my own devise.

I'll think of slowing, stopping the car,
crunching on a pebbled shoulder,
breasting through black thickets toward them.
I'll steal through bracken fern and scouring rush,
fairyslipper, salal and velvetgrass,
saying the names as if conjuring them,
far back, pressing into wilderness,
hands sticky with sap and berry-juice,
sniffing essences, tugging roots,
hunting for a memory of white;
until I'll find, beneath sprouting mayweed,
like a gift I'd been expecting,
in a clearing, by moonlight,
a flaked-off sheet of birch-bark,
light as air, a fraying mesh:

a blank endpaper come loose
turning past a story's final page;
the lesson I am always having to learn
word by word, and all by heart.

DAVID GRAVENDER

A Friendly and Equitable Insurance

I've been out in the woods and brought something home.
A creature, no, nor lichen sleeved from a branch.
I've been digging, not to lay a ghost
or to find a father, but to uncover the taproot
of that famous tree from the book of memory.
I post myself a report on its territory:
a nervous system of root, the brain of leaf,
perennial synapses of forgettings and rememberings.
And when I receive it I will not believe in it;
but bin it with my father and all the creatures,
dead or imagined, not worth the risk,
a risk which could make me hate myself.

The next morning I will not go to the woods.
I'll read about my death by easy payments.
For if my eyelash offends I pluck it.
If the city grows too hot I leave it,
hitting the countryside with its big-hearted hedges,
vistas and many sites of historical interest.
In everything I do, I offend something.
The taproot oozes oil, spreads across my memory,
blacks and confuses it. I must do as I please
with this sunlit morning: the light is accurate
and I stand square as though I owned it.
As though I deserved it no more.

DAVID MORLEY

Winterwood

Through treble-thick stone converted
stable walls I hear a horse canter in puddles
– close-up – bidden slow
at temporary lights on the cobbled way.
Night-bus headlamps sweep drystone
walling. Stark with no passengers
to speak of. A relief driver focuses hard
on the hill-edge poplar windbreak;
awaits the blur of amber; glances
night-skyward, tense with unpredictable hemispheres,
the aligning of planets. And you reach out to me
in the sealed dark of our windowless world,
have me stroke the back of your neck
as I emerge from companies of village ghosts
that follow and find me, far from home
on a street where I've never been,
alighting perhaps from a lit bus that slowed
but never stopped. We slip soundly,
waken to coachouse quiet and the hush of crows.

ANNE–MARIE FYFE

Blackthorn Winter

Late rain drove them all from the stableyard.
Gina's old thoroughbred, stiff in blue rugs,
Carla's iron-grey Carmen (who whinnies, tugs,
Though only waist-high) snatched hay, then stared.
While jeeps, a battered van beat a retreat,
The pony trotted me through the dusk's sleet.

Tender white glow on the circle of hills
Whirled into snow, soaked the mud from my sleeves,
Darkened the tips of the pony's small ears.
We galloped down tracks. No sight of a bird
Or living soul met us. Icy mud blurred
Into our faces. The feeble bulb spilled

Green on the hay I crammed into her rack
From the storm of the dark. Everything fell
In the unseen mud, key, gloves, soaked towel.
Then strange windows glimmered behind my back,
My car: furred snow-soft. No stars filled the dead
Eye of the sky, blind with flake. I, too, fled.

It skimmed the slope where small houses once lay,
The first, lost village. As swift as the snow
It was a hare. It was vast. It dropped low
Into feathers of white. The great ears reared,
It bounded out of my beam, then careered
To hedge-holes, brambles, to wait for wet day.

How long is an evening? Who would have thought,
After all this, that a main traffic light
Would freeze on red; so I had to swing right
In the small town, where the snow had now thawed
To a sharp iced rain, to wander the grounds
Of dark, new bungalows, where I turned round.

Lost in a courtyard, I wrenched the wheel right.
Behind warm windows from ceiling to floor
Hunched and alert, the men watched me. I saw
One spin a wheelchair. Under their glass
Sheltered from mud and ice, soaring but fast,
White hyacinths opened into the made light.

ALISON BRACKENBURY

Blue Gentian

It shone in alpine tundra near the cable-car summit
Held by NATO. Such a deep dark blue, so sudden
And isolated, it made me think at once of being somewhere

Deep as love, as it came to me, then wonder if it was the same
As in D. H. Lawrence, a blue match-flame igniting
The paisley tussocks and mosses whorled by mushrooms

In some grain of high-energy inwardness. I took it
To check, in a field guide, if I had found the poetry of the real
Thing held tensile as dew's quicksilver trembling

In the rare globe of its pronunciation. When we reached
the perimeter wire, the French guard watched us descend
Near the twisted deck of the meteorological station

Whose German founder's lone Gothic gravestone lay below,
And where you could imagine it would be better than a hospital to die –
In so far as death might ring the curtain, at least, on one last

Moment of utter beauty. So that when we kept descending
The serpentine road where the transport rose
To pass us, into a sudden strange light from the western cloud-front,

That time stayed with me...

CHRIS AGEE

The Bøya Glacier

Eerily blue like a cascade from heaven,
a cold light captured between summers,

it wedges between the sheen of the sky
and shattered grey mountains,
its inching glass suspended over my head.

A sign shouts silently *Danger! Glaciers
are in motion!* I listen for a tell-tale creak
in the depths, the sly creep of death,

as if the Ice Age still looms here,
a blue-grey wolf hunkered on the rocks
easing its bulk into August's green glade.

With caution I scan the dank shale at its edge,
black grit of moraine, pink helliborine
startling the snow, meltwater dripping

small coins all day with slow grief;
and I look again at the glacier's height,
the just-glimpsed body of frozen light,

a dying hand flung down the valley,
a sweat of diamonds vanishing as I watch.

LYNNE WYCHERLEY

Gondolier

As we drove down from mountains
into the Skagit floodplain, poised
    for just a moment near a weigh station
    in a slow bend of freeway,
                      her voice
lifting and dropping was a hawk
    measuring its flight, while through my window
    I could just make out
        in the open distance ahead

a tall balloon burgeoning into view, resisting
    the tug of earth, breathing high
      over a mud-rutted smudge of stubble,
    the whiff of fresh manure.

The size of my thumb, it hung
    low in a bare museum of sky
    painted bright blue and yellow,
                  burning furiously
    to hold itself in an equilibrium
    between inertia and pure flight:

                a mind
neither awake nor unawake; a question
    in the white pause before
    even the hope of an answer;
a dream as it lingers
    just beyond the day's literal reach,
    scented of flowers whose names
        are always drifting away, evaporating
    on the tip of the tongue,
              into thin air.

So arrive my daylight hauntings, the shapes
        I rise to, impressions, suggestions,
                the invisible currents I would gauge
like a gondolier lofted in an open basket
        quizzing the winds, dependent
                on the elements at hand, a pilot
                of middle space, ballasted
                        in an unseen tension,
                        a holding pattern, a judgment
                                in evolution, in panoply:
                                                a reminiscence
        of what may be, a prediction about
        what has been:

a phoenix as it might conceive
        the life it knew before the pyre,
                                        eternity
        reduced to the taste of ash and apples,
        bitter and familiar;

the moon's ghost,
        reflective, gazing over a shoulder,
                                        releasing
        its slim tether to dream
                deep in earth's faceless
                        atmosphere of blue;

she and I, flying down the road,
        in the wide lull of conversation,
                embarked on one more day
                of being alone together
                        with only the wind
                and what burden it
                        might carry.

DAVID GRAVENDER

Above Middleton

From this hill the view is larger than God,
the weather less forgiving.

Rough land, honed by a battering wind
that thrums over the houses
and howls inside the head like a chained dog.

This is the cold that cracks stone,
breaks open keens on calloused fingers
for the few descendants of the long-forgotten dead

who moled the lead seams under the Pennines,
leaving their poisoned bones
in unmarked graves.

Their cottages are fallen stone
and the roofless church
has a congregation of nettles.

They lived, not without language
or music, or the violence
of loving and birthing and hunger.

Only a death brought them down,
ill-suited in their mildewed best
to walk twelve miles to church –

buried, christened, married in job lots.
Crossing their brief marks against the register
of unrecorded lives.

Even their work is hidden
in pipes, drains, the linings of coffins,
or beaten flat in the gutters

of redundant churches, divers' boots,
the hems of old velvet curtains, fishermen's weights,
the deadly interior of a nuclear flask.

KATHLEEN JONES

Gasometer

I used to run past Gas Street, afraid
the merest whim would spark it off. It loomed green
over everything, the garlic smell warning
of strange powers. It went up and down
like moods, the whole town lit up and cooking.

The North Sea bubble blew it out.
Around the country, empty gantries lingered
beyond notice on the skyline, rusting and redundant,
to be wrenched apart by economic forces,
oxy-torches and an engine with a shear.

Which is why I'm up here, nose-down on this dome
where they're peeling back the skin: rivet-dimpled,
with blooms of colour where the torch has cut.
Paint flakes and catches underneath my nails.
Unconcealed, the tank goes deeper than I'd thought.

The edge I'm leaning on creaks slightly
but it's warm in the sun as my camera gropes
for the secrets of its structure, how in the dark
it swelled with power on a raft of water and floated up
to the very top. This broken, empty thing – I want

it whole again, the spokes and posts re-covered
as the welders left them, sealed under me and rising...
Guide-wheels squeak up pillars and in the yard
they're shovelling coke, and gas is filling darkness
half an inch below me, lifting me into the view.

ANNE BERKELEY

Going Under

Already at the brink he could have gone in storm, raging
under its electric dagger, naked, phosphorous, blue,
his body flickering into conflict, responding
to commands of Thunder, the God rising in his blood
streaming out beyond the known cone of himself.
In storm he would have descended violently,
bull-roaring at annihilation, bruising fists
hammering the green glass gates of Manannan's palaces
until the locks of dulse and wrack broke open
and he jack-knifed through,
the undertow wound round his body like a guiding rope.

Or did he chose a day like this – a grace of light
silver on the tide? He could have walked into the river
at the estuary's long loop
between tiers of blazing gorse where larks spiral out to heaven
and mossy boulders hold the empty cave of ram's white ribs
as an archway for the bees.   Going out with the tide

he could have followed the wake of blue-legged swans
stately as burial barges, his hands grown frond-like
trailing nets through the river's speed, spread toes
tender to the peaty ooze, his face
still within the realm of real time; one white feather
coming back to him, and passing.

Only water was open for him now he was deafened to earth,
to air. At the edge the waves' cadenza
drowned the plover's alarm, the shrilling of oyster catchers;
only the seagull's screams reached him, and tore him.
Black-plumed cormorants flew a line of nine
and one stood as an angel pointing deep
as the Sea took him, hushing his cries, soothing
the salt from his skin   his eyes –

                    Going under
that glittery silver light became milky and he could sleep.
Gently then his memoried cells unfolded
like paper water-flowers finding their release.

Afterwards he would only shrug and say some luck of wind
had turned a sail towards him.
He was changed of course. I saw that his hands had opened out
and he held his palms wide as if both receiving and letting go,
whatever the weather. I would say he prospered, late in life
began to paint, loved again, grew tangerines.

ROSE FLINT

Taste

Vita exits a taxi.
A spark released from coal
or petals pushed from a black bud sheath:
her fine-tulle skirt
satsuma-orange,
chrysanthemum, tangelo, gerbera, marigold...
a flash of tropical in the storm,
she runs up the gallery steps in the rain.

Later, tells us that night she dreamed a coughing fit:
Rita Angus paintings leapt from her mouth,
eloquent palettes, bright, speechless balloons.

Which reminds Daniel to offer whisky.
Hot honeyed apple, with a sting,
or wild, smoke-swept, a campfire on the highlands,
or clover-spiced, peaty, malty?

Vita says, like her grandmother once,
"Mine tastes of bells rung under sea."
Justin savours, swallows.
They tingle and hum beneath his tongue:
all his words, that want to cluster to her,
like bees to ink made of grenadine
or to the sweet, peeled skin
of mandarins, tangerines.

EMMA NEALE

Tres Pechugas

In this town of sugar skulls, a church designed
by a ten year old from an Italian postcard,
Susannah has given up painting altogether.
Instead she mixes papier-mâché, forms
creased, yellowing bodies, naked rib cages.

In this town you can buy tiny silver limbs:
an ear, an elbow, a stretched out hand
to avoid illness. All over her clothes
Susannah stitches them, biting off
crimson thread with her teeth.

Evenings, she walks up Calle Reloj,
three necklaces heavy about her throat,
past the tortilleria, the shop interior
crème de menthe, with a silver machine
spitting tortillas hot and flat as summer sky.

She buys chicken legs and breasts for her Texan lover,
who, omnipotent belly up, watches CNN and pretends
he's elsewhere. 'Tres pechugas y tres piernas por favor',
she says with a childish lilt. And the men stare
at her waist cinched in with a gold bead-belt.

Susannah's house is in the old quarter –
and when she enters, the man calling for his dinner
there's a lizard; tongue flickering
a brief candle flame, body a large black seed
against the watermelon walls.

PAOLA BILBROUGH

Amaretti
for my father

Toadstool-tops — two, cracked as nana's old
knee sore. And you launched one towards
the ceiling, white ridge-beam of your mouth
waiting, barely budged your chin to grind it
like a roof-tile; offered the other, pathetic
as a button on your outstretched palm. And I
snatched it quick as a whisker, bit, felt my tongue
melt caverns deep inside, release its acrid-sweet
almond adultness –
          which I dribbled out, in spite
of the almost-shake of your loaf, the high arches
of your brows. Then you tunnelled the wrapper
between fingers to roll a joke, a giant's
cigarillo from air's tobacco; stood it
end-first on ma's stainless tea-tray, flicked
your flint lighter to chase the tip with flame
which seeped downwards, filled my head
with burning –
          until, at the last,
it wobbled, transfigured, a ganglion
of desire there, rose up into our cathedralled
Italian stairwell: willed-wisp of your making
who stood, an edifice of father frowning
his gargoyled wonder into mine, our wish
held up by ash, all trembling, climbing
into hallowed space.

MARIO PETRUCCI

Notes on contributors

The locations in parenthesis indicate current place of residence.

CHRIS AGEE (Belfast) teaches American Studies at The Open University in Ireland. A first collection, *In The New Hampshire Woods*, was published by Dedalus in 1992; a second, *First Light,* has just been completed. He edited *Scar on the Stone: Contemporary Poetry From Bosnia* (Bloodaxe, 1998), a PBS Recommendation. A collection of Balkan essays, *Journey to Bosnia*, will appear later this year.

JILL BAMBER (London) was a Blue Nose Poet of the Year in 1998. She has previously won the London Writers and the National Poetry Foundation Competitions and is the author of five verse collections, most recently *Flying Blind* (National Poetry Foundation, 2000).

ANNE BERKELEY (Cambridge) has had many poems published in magazines. Flarestack published a pamphlet, *The Buoyancy Aid and Other Poems,* in 1997.

PAOLA BILBROUGH (Brunswick, Australia) has had work published in the UK in *Stand* and *The London Magazine.* Her first collection of poems, *Bell Tongue*, was published by Victoria University Press (NZ) in 1999. She has a writing fellowship at Keio University in Tokyo this year, where she will be working on a novel.

ALISON BRACKENBURY (Gloucestershire) has published five collections of poetry. The most recent is *After Beethoven* (Carcanet, 2000).

LAWRENCE BRADY (Crosby, Merseyside) has lectured in History and Art History and has published a biography of the politician and journalist T. P. O'Connor (1983). He has studied painting with the Open College of the Arts and has been a prize-winner in the College's national competition.

CAROLE BROMLEY (York) has had poems published in a number of magazines including *Stand, The Rialto* and *Smiths Knoll.* She won first prize in the *Staple Open Poetry Competition* and *First Lines* in 2000 and was runner-up for the Housman Prize. She is currently working on her first collection.

WAYNE BURROWS (London) has a first collection, *Marginalia*, just out from Peterloo. His book on the work of artist Sarah Lucas, *With Knobs On...*, is available from PAVIC/Culture Matters. He works as a freelance editor with The Literary Consultancy.

STEPHEN BURT (Minnesota) is assistant professor of English at Macalester College in St. Paul, Minnesota, where he is completing a book about Randall Jarrell. His book of poems, *Popular Music*, won the Colorado Prize for 1999; some of its work can also be found in *New Poetries II* (Carcanet).

IAN CAWS (West Sussex) has published nine collections of poetry, including *The Ragman Totts* (Redcliffe, 1990) – a PBS Recommendation – and, most recently, *Dialogues in Mask* (Pikestaff, 2000).

POLLY CLARK (Oxford) works in publishing. A former Eric Gregory Award winner, her first collection, *Kiss* (Bloodaxe, 2000), was a PBS recommendation.

JULIA COPUS (Blackburn) won a PBS Recommendation for her first book, *The Shuttered Eye* (Bloodaxe, 1995). She is currently completing her second collection.

ROSE FLINT (Bath) teaches creative writing and is an art therapist. Her poems have appeared in numerous magazines, including *Poetry Review*, *Poetry Wales* and *Acumen*. Her first collection is *Blue Horse of Morning* (Seren).

LINDA FRANCE (Northumberland) is the editor of *Sixty Women Poets* (1993) and the author of the volumes *Red* (1992), *The Gentleness of the Very Tall* (1994) and *Storyville* (1997), all from Bloodaxe. A new collection, *The Simultaneous Dress*, is due in 2002.

ANNE-MARIE FYFE (London) runs Coffee-House Poetry at The Troubadour in Earls Court, teaches poetry at Richmond Adult College and is a freelance creative-writing tutor. Her poems have won prizes in the Arvon, Peterloo, Bridport and Kent & Sussex competitions and are published in *Late Crossing* (Rockingham, 1999). A second collection is due in October 2001.

JUDY GAHAGAN (London) won first prize in the Peterloo Competition 2000. She is a freelance writer and translator and runs seminars and tutorials with the Poetry School in London. Her most recent verse collection, *Crossing The No-Man's Land*, was published by Flambard in 1999.

DAVID GRAVENDER (Seattle) is a former *Tabla* prize-winner and E.J. Pratt Poetry Award recipient. His work has appeared in *The Fiddlehead*, *Queen's Quarterly* and previous *Tabla* anthologies. He is currently looking to publish a first collection.

EAMON GRENNAN (New York) is the Dexter M. Ferry Jr. Professor of English at Vassar College. His most recent publications are *Relations: New & Selected Poems* (Graywolf, 1998), *Leopardi: Selected Poems* (Princeton University Press, 1997), and a collection of critical essays, *Facing the Music: Irish Poetry in the Twentieth Century* (Creighton University Press, 1999). In Ireland, Gallery Press recently published his *Selected & New Poems*.

KATHLEEN JONES (Cumbria) is a full-time writer. Her publications include a biography of Catherine Cookson and *A Passionate Sisterhood* (Virago), the lives of the sisters, wives and daughters of the 'Lake' poets. Her most recent poetry collection is *Unwritten Lives* (Redbeck).

KHAN SINGH KUMAR (Surrey) explores issues to do with Asians living in the west in many of his poems. His work has been published in *Poetry Review*, *PN Review*, *Stand*, *Poetry London*, *Poetry Ireland*, *New Writing 10* and *Magma*.

MEDBH MCGUCKIAN (Belfast) is in charge of the MA in Poetry Writing at Queen's University, Belfast. Her books, including a *Selected Poems*, are available from Gallery Press in Ireland and Wake Forest Press in The United States.

DAVID MORLEY (Warwick) directs the Writing Programme at the University of Warwick. He has received a major Eric Gregory Award, an Arts Council Writers Award and an Arts Council Fellowship. He co-edited *The New Poetry* for Bloodaxe. His work has appeared in The British Council's *New Writing* and Faber's *Poetry Introduction* anthologies.

EMMA NEALE (Dunedin, New Zealand) is a freelance editor and writer. Her new novel, *Little Moon*, is out with Vintage (NZ) in the middle of 2001.

KATHERINE PAGE (Middlesex) works as the research director for the National Readership Survey. Some of her poems appear in the new *Blodeuwedd* anthology (Headland, 2000).

M. R. PEACOCKE (Cumbria) lives and works on a hill farm and practises as a counsellor. Peterloo have published two collections of her poems: *Marginal Land* (1988) and *Selves* (1995).

MARIO PETRUCCI (Enfield), physicist, ecologist, songwriter and twice-winner of the London Writers Competition, is currently an RLF Fellow at Oxford Brookes University and a tutor for the Poetry Society's 'Poetryclass' initiative. *Shrapnel and Sheets* is available from Headland and *Bosco* from Hearing Eye.

SALLY READ (London) has had several poems published in British magazines and is represented in the *Blodeuwedd* anthology (Headland, 2000). She is currently working towards her first collection.

LEONIE RUSHFORTH (London) teaches English, has written reviews and articles for various magazines and is just beginning to publish poetry.

ROBERT SAXTON (London) works in illustrated book publishing. He is a regular contributor to *Poetry Review* and his work has also appeared in the *TLS*, *The Observer*, *PN Review*, *The Paris Review* and *London Magazine*. A first collection, *The Promise Clinic*, appeared from Enitharmon in 1994 and a second, *Bottomfishing*, is nearing completion.

ROBERT SEATTER (London) will appear in *Anvil New Poets III* (spring 2001). He has been a prize-winner twice in the National Poetry Competition and four times in *Tabla's* own contest. He also won first prize in the 2000 *Poetry London* competition. He works at the BBC.

HENRY SHUKMAN (Warwickshire), an ex-trawlerman, toilet-cleaner and professional trombonist, is now a travel-writer. He recently won *The Daily Telegraph* Arvon Poetry Prize, a *Times Literary Supplement* Poetry Prize and an Arts Council of England Writer's Award.

IAN STARSMORE (Norfolk) is a painter, printmaker and writer. He was the originator of the Cultural Studies courses at Norwich School of Art and now teaches for the Open University.

GEORGE SZIRTES (Norfolk) is the author of fourteen volumes of poetry, including *The Budapest File* (Bloodaxe, 2000) and *An English Apocalypse* (forthcoming). He writes regular book reviews for *The Times* and is working on a monograph about the artist Ana Maria Pacheco. A book of translations from the Hungarian poet Agnes Nemes Nagy is also in the pipeline.

HOWARD WRIGHT (Belfast) lectures in Art History at the University of Ulster at Belfast. He was a runner-up in the Bridport Prize 2000 and his poems have appeared in *Stand*, *The North*, *The Irish University Review* and *Writing Ulster: Northern Narratives*. A pamphlet collection, *Usquebaugh*, was published by the Redbeck Press in 1997.

LYNNE WYCHERLEY (Oxfordshire) is a keen environmentalist and has won an award for rural poetry. A former Blue Nose Poet-of-the-Year, her pamphlet collections are *Cracks in the Ice* (Acumen, 1999) and *A Sea of Dark Fields* (Hilton House, 2000).

Back issues

Previous volumes of The Tabla Book of New Verse are now available for only £2 each or £3 for any two or £4 for all three – while stocks last. Prices include postage. For overseas orders, please add £1.00 (Europe) or £2.00 (rest of world) per book.

Cheques and postal orders should be made payable to Tabla. Only UK *sterling payments can be accepted.*

The Tabla Book of New Verse 2000 includes poems by

Chris Agee	Rose Flint	Andrew Neilson
John Allison	Judy Gahagan	James Norcliffe
Cliff Ashcroft	Louise Glück	Katherine Page
Jill Bamber	David Gravender	Sally Read
Ros Barber	Philip Gross	Mark Roper
Chris Beckett	Kerry Hardie	Robert Saxton
Wayne Burrows	Allison Eir Jenks	Robert Seatter
Peter Carpenter	Andrew Johnston	Henry Shukman
Ian Caws	John Kinsella	John Stammers
Paul F. Cowlan	W. S. Merwin	Anne Stevenson
Martyn Crucefix	Art Murphy	Howard Wright

The Tabla Book of New Verse 1999 includes poems by

Jill Bamber	David Gravender	Maggie O'Farrell
Paola Bilbrough	David Hartnett	Katherine Page
John Burnside	Jane Holland	Mario Petrucci
Stephen Burt	Andrew Johnston	Peter Redgrove
Peter Carpenter	Kathleen Jones	Mark Roper
Paul F. Cowlan	Mimi Khalvati	Robert Seatter
Rose Flint	John Knowles	Pauline Stainer
Judy Gahagan	James Norcliffe	Charles Tomlinson
Sydney Giffard	Rosemary Norman	Howard Wright

and prose

Peter McDonald on Seamus Heaney and Michael Longley

Steven Matthews on Pauline Stainer

John Burnside on David Gravender

Samantha Matthews: finding poetry

Peter Carpenter and David Morley: mapping poetry

Mario Petrucci: distributing poetry

Carol Rumens in interview

The Tabla Book of New Verse 1998 includes poems by

Gillian Allnutt	Giles Goodland	Peter McDonald
Jill Bamber	David Gravender	Paul Muldoon
Chris Beckett	Vona Groarke	Emma Neale
Matthew Caley	Paul Groves	Katherine Page
Peter Carpenter	Kerry Hardie	Cate Parish
Polly Clark	Tobias Hill	Mario Petrucci
Peter Daniels	Andrew Johnston	Robin Robertson
Jane Duran	Andrew Jordan	Mark Roper
Lynne Elson	Martha Kapos	Robert Seatter
Rose Flint	Marion Lomax	Michael Tolkien

and prose

Peter McDonald on Robin Robertson

Mark Willis on Derek Walcott

Andrew Johnston on Peter Carpenter

*Good homes are also sought for the remaining unsold copies of
Tabla poetry magazine no. 6 (1997).*

*This includes work by, among others, Jill Bamber, Peter Carpenter,
Rose Flint, Judy Gahagan, David Gravender, Seamus Heaney,
Peter McDonald, Maggie O'Farrell, Ruth Padel, Carol Rumens
and Robert Seatter, plus reviews of Tobias Hill, Paul Muldoon and
John Kinsella.*

*If you would like a free copy, please send in a self-addressed A5 envelope
with stamps to the value of 44 pence to cover second class UK postage.*

Issues 1-5 of the magazine (1992-96) are now sold out.

Eleventh annual *Tabla* poetry competition

JUDGE: GEORGES SZIRTES
CLOSING DATE: 31.07.2001

- There will be a first prize of £500, a second prize of £200 and three runner-up awards of £100 each.

- These and other selected entrants will have their work published in *The Tabla Book of New Verse 2002*.

- Those who have bought a copy of this year's book may enter one poem in the competition free of charge. (Please send a sales receipt as proof of purchase.) Further entries and entries by those not purchasing the book cost £3.00 each.

- Copies of *The Tabla Book of New Verse 2001* cost £6.00 each (post free). For overseas orders, please add £1.00 (Europe) or £2.00 (rest of world).

- Cheques and postal orders should be made payable to *Tabla* (UK sterling only).

- Poems may be of any length, preferably typed and on A4 paper. They should not bear the author's name. E-mail entries cannot be accepted, nor can entries be returned.

- Each entry must be the unaided work of the author. It should not have been published or broadcast previously.

- The minimum age for entry is sixteen.

- Please remember to enclose the requisite SAE(s) for receipt of entry and/or notification of results (if desired).

- Poems and payments may be submitted directly but for an official entry form send an SAE (or IRC) to the editorial address; alternatively, print one off the *Tabla* website: www.bristol.ac.uk/tabla